IMAGES OF WILDNESS

NEW JERSEY

TOM TILL

FOREWORD BY SENATOR BILL BRADLEY

WESTCLIFFE PUBLISHERS, INC. ENGLEWOOD, COLORADO

CONTENTS

International Standard Book Number: ISBN 0-929969-42-1
Library of Congress Catalogue Card Number: 90-071520
Copyright, Photographs and Text: Tom Till, 1991.
    All rights reserved.
Copyright, Foreword: Bill Bradley, 1991.
Editor: John Fielder
Assistant Editor: Margaret Terrell Morse
Production Manager: Mary Jo Lawrence
Typographers: Dianne Borneman and Ruth Koning
Printed in Hong Kong by Dai Nippon Printing Company,
    Ltd., Tokyo, Japan
Published by Westcliffe Publishers, Inc.
    2650 South Zuni Street, Englewood, Colorado 80110

Bibliography

Selections from *The Pine Barrens* by John McPhee. Copyright
    © 1968 by John McPhee. Reprinted by permission of
    Farrar, Straus & Giroux, Inc.
Whitman, Walt. *Specimen Days*. New York: The Viking Press,
    Literary Classics of the United States, *Complete Prose
    Works*, 1982.

First Frontispiece: Sunrise light on palisades above
    the Hudson River, Palisades Interstate Park
Second Frontispiece: Sycamores in snow, Wharton
    State Forest, Pine Barrens
Title Page: Morning fog drifts through trees in the
    Appalachian Mountains, Delaware Water Gap
    National Recreation Area
Third Frontispiece: Looking south over Delaware Bay
    at sunset; Cape May County.
Right: Daisies in morning light, near the Delaware River

BILL BRADLEY
FOREWORD

Before automobile plants, steel mills, computer terminals, there was the land. Before our nation was even 10 years old, Thomas Jefferson looked around him and began to worry about open space. Philadelphia was a teeming metropolis — 70,000 people lived there. New York was closing in — 60,000 people. Even in the countryside, Jefferson was alarmed to find a density of 10 people per square mile.

In New Jersey, there are more than 1,000 people per square mile. In some counties, it's 12,000 per square mile. Many of us live by the schedule of commuter trains. If we slow down, it's only because we're caught in a traffic jam. We're surrounded by noise, not the sound of wind and rain, but the noise of machines. Yet we still need the land, not for the material wealth it provides, but for a sense of who we are — individually and as a people. And in New Jersey, we still have the land.

One spring day I visited Batsto, a village in the Pine Barrens that seems like it's from another era. There I climbed a fire tower to look out from above the surroundings. From horizon to horizon, the world was green, a lawn of pine and cypress. In that early spring air, I could sense the reawakening, the renewal of growth. On that day, the wilderness in front of me represented the hope and promise of the future.

The Pine Barrens are a natural miracle that connects one of the most densely populated metropolitan stretches of America with a different kind of life, a life lived according to the rhythms of the natural world. Twenty percent of the state — 1.1 million acres — is protected, much of it a rich, pristine wilderness of scrub pines and wetlands. It is the kind of landscape that writer Barry Lopez has described as "two landscapes — one outside the self, the other within." The interior landscape "responds to the character and subtlety of the exterior one; the shape of the individual mind is affected by land as it is by genes."

The Pine Barrens are such a unique environmental treasure that they have been designated by the United Nations as an International Biosphere Reserve, a rare distinction they share with Yellowstone National Park and the Florida Everglades. But they are not the only natural miracle of New Jersey that comes to life in Tom Till's photographs. The Jersey shore — stretching from the Twin Lights at Sandy Hook along 120 miles of narrow islands to the Victorian seaside town of Cape May and then around the point to 300-year-old towns like Salem and Greenwich — become a part of nearly every New Jersey family's life in the summer. And in the northwestern portion of the state, The Delaware River carves out a low valley that is as varied in its scenery as any in America.

"Wilderness can't grow. It can only shrink," Aldo Leopold has said. In New Jersey, perhaps because so many of us live so close together, we understand this troubling fact and have worked for years to preserve every acre of open space we can for our children and grandchildren. The land is our teacher. It instructs us in the value of things that can't be bought or sold, traded or exchanged. in our encounters with the land we are in touch with something that is larger than we are and that lasts longer than we do.

In these fine color photographs, you will discover the richness and the wildness of the land that makes life in New Jersey unique, unexpected and wonderful.

— BILL BRADLEY
U.S. Senator, New Jersey

Left: Buttermilk Falls descends stone terraces, Delaware Water Gap National Recreation Area
Overleaf: Autumn canopy of Stokes State Forest at dawn, from Sunrise Point

TOM TILL

PREFACE

As I talked with people around the country about my work on a book of photos portraying the natural beauty of New Jersey, I received a number of interesting reactions. Most people, including a great number of natives to the state, know very little about the incredible richness, diversity and beauty of New Jersey's natural legacy. Some I spoke with scoffed at the idea of wilderness or untouched natural areas in the state. They held to the popular notion that New Jersey is a polluted wasteland, besmirched from one border to the other by toxic waste, oil slicks, factory smoke and endless turnpikes. Others, a little more familiar with the state, fell into the opposing camp. "Well, you know there are some beautiful areas there," they maintained, enjoying their contradiction of the prevailing image.

When I began this project, I was as ignorant as anyone. Although I had done a great deal of nature photography in the eastern United States, my interests and prejudices had taken me to areas better known for their scenic beauty. Nonetheless, I was confident I could find plenty to photograph even in a state much maligned as an ecological disaster. What surprised me was how inspired and excited I was by what I found. As I finished my work I was still discovering interesting new places to photograph and explore.

Having said this, I do not want to produce the illusion with these photographs that New Jersey's natural environment is secure and unimperiled. You may see air pollution, encroaching housing subdivisions, and even beer cans and garbage in these pictures if you look closely. My intent is not to create a fairy-tale vision, but to champion the resiliency and magnificence of a beleaguered heritage.

During my travels around the state I spent a lot of time searching for rock formations unadorned with spray paint. At one lovely viewpoint in the Delaware Water Gap I found a fine group of outcroppings along spectacular Kittatinny Ridge. I was so impressed with their magnificence and the almost western ruggedness of the scene that I decided to return at dawn the following day to continue my work. To my horror, the early morning light revealed that many of the boulders had been spray painted and vandalized overnight. My sorrow and disappointment stemmed not from the loss of a photographic opportunity, but from the significance of the act. Although the vandals were probably just foolish drunks, I see them as a symbol of our estrangement from, and lack of respect for, our natural heritage.

Over the years, many areas of New Jersey have drawn me back again and again to hike and photograph. Delaware Water Gap National Recreation Area, rightfully given national recognition by its establishment in 1965, is one of the loveliest mountain areas of the East. Almost within sight of one of the world's largest metropolitan areas, the Appalachian Mountains are split by the sinuous Delaware River. Once called the Eighth Wonder of the World, the Water Gap area deserves national park designation, with management decisions based on full protection of its unique beauty.

Although the river and valleys in this area are stunning, I was particularly attracted by the hollows and ravines that lead back from the river to the mountaintops. As abundant rain and snow fall on the high ridges of the Water Gap, dozens of spectacular waterfalls are born and quickly relinquish themselves to the river. Some are transitory, coming and going rapidly after storms. One raw December day after an especially wet spell, I saw numerous cascades streaming down ridges, turning an entire flank of a hillside into one nearly continuous falls. A cold snap added more magic, decorating each rushing stream with a coating of ice sculpture.

These copious waters also feed the finest natural rock gardens I've ever seen. While exploring a forest trail in May I glimpsed a flash of brilliant color through the thick woods. A short walk brought me to a stony wall adorned with columbine and trillium. High above me the profusion and color of flowers reached even greater glories, with gigantic clumps of flora blanketing the cliff face. Though I spent all morning climbing from above and below, I could find no way to approach the flowers with a camera. Slippery rock faces and the precipitous cliffs kept me away, able to admire the displays only from a distance. Perhaps that's why the garden had thrived. It had been forever safe from the intrusions of flower pickers and photographers.

East of the Water Gap the mountains continue, almost to the sea. I was continually eager to hike the trails in the many fine state parks and forests of this region, with their exquisite lakes and craggy boulder peaks. The summits of the Ramapo Mountains nearly all afford a view of the New York City skyline, but I was still taken aback when I passed through a handsome pine and birch forest reminiscent of northern Minnesota, only to read a sign that announced "Newark, 26 Miles."

The New Jersey Pine Barrens, another area I grew to love, is one of America's most enchanting regions. Having visited

Left: Spring forest with azalea in full bloom, Somerset County

most of our country's wildlands, I can truly say that the Pine Barrens is unique. Languid lily-padded lakes, thick primeval forest and slowly moving, inky black streams, as clear, paradoxically, as any Colorado brook characterize this wilderness managed by the state and federal governments.

I spent many nights in the Pine Barrens, often with storms, rain or even tornadoes to keep things interesting. At times I was a little homesick for the western landscape, as the pine-scented air reminded me of the North Rim of the Grand Canyon and the Uinta Mountains of Utah. Oftentimes I found myself thinking about the New Jersey landscape of 20, 50 or even 100 years ago. What a beautiful land it must have been for our ancestors. At one prime vantage point in the Pine Barrens it's possible to look out on an almost totally wild 360-degree panorama and to have the illusion of seeing the forests as they must have appeared generations ago. The work of groups such as the Pinelands Commission will go far toward ensuring that the Pine Barrens' wild character will be preserved intact for future generations to enjoy.

The ocean is never far away in New Jersey. A place of splendor and untamed beauty, it is also the site of one of America's most publicized environmental disasters. Although I saw no medical wastes along the Jersey Shore, the amount of trash was depressing, especially at places like Sandy Hook. I'm not an oceanographer, and I'm sure there are more pressing ocean pollution problems than garbage washed up on shore, but this is one cleanup task that should receive top priority from our government and private citizens. The Earth Day 1990 pickup of Sandy Hook was a great effort, with Tri-State–area people showing their firm commitment to improving the shore environment. Ridding all of New Jersey's natural attractions of waste, though, will require an education program to renew respect for our land and our ocean resources.

My most memorable trip to the shore coincided with a major autumn storm. I had visited Island Beach State Park on many occasions without taking a single photo. Bad weather and gales had forced me back to the mainland every time. Undaunted, I arrived as the rain ended and the storm moved offshore, providing me a glimpse of the Atlantic at its most furious. Conditions were impossible for my large format 4x5 camera, so I spent one of my most exhilarating days in New Jersey dodging sneaker waves and breakers with a smaller format camera.

By contrast, a perfectly calm day with a very low tide at Sandy Hook was the scene for one of my most productive photographic experiences. It was one of those days that come from time to time when I need to exert little effort. Photograph after photograph revealed itself to me, each one a great gift. As sunset approached — *magic hour* as photographers often refer to it — I had more photographic ideas than I could possibly render in the time remaining. I will never forget that day and the joy and harmony I felt while working there.

The Great Swamp, Hudson Palisades, Ken Lockwood Gorge, Watchung Mountains and Jenny Jump State Forest are just a few of the many nature preserves I visited while working on these photographs. It is my hope that these images will serve as a reminder of the natural world struggling to persist around the margins of urban America. The work of the state of New Jersey and many of its citizens to preserve and protect natural areas and wildlife, to pass and enforce tough environmental laws, and to educate the public about our wild heritage can serve as an example for many other states.

In one of the world's most densely populated areas, New Jersey's wild and natural areas take on great value and significance. With fewer and fewer places to retreat from more and more civilization, our remaining pristine lands stand like endangered species. If they can survive and thrive in New Jersey, perhaps we can gain hope from them for our nation and our world.

— TOM TILL

The photographs in this book are dedicated to the memory of Eliot Porter.

Left: Moss-covered tree beside the South Branch of the Raritan River, Ken Lockwood Gorge, New Jersey Highlands

COLOR

Color is a key compositional tool for the landscape photographer. Our eyes can discern tens of thousands of shadings and nuances of colors, and most evoke an emotional response.

Lighting is a key factor in this alchemy. Early morning sun bursting through a cloud bank on Kittatinny Mountain may momentarily bathe the subject in light as crimson as the showiest maple leaf. On cloudy or rainy days, colors of nearby objects may be far more intense and vibrant than when it's sunny.

Film can surprise us by showing colors that our eyes have seen but our brains have overlooked, only to be revealed in the final photograph.

Seasonal color in New Jersey's forest country provides a wide and diverse palette. Winter offers subtle monochromatic variations on the same theme. Only the intense red light of a crisp clear morning or a sunset provides an infusion of warm colors. In summer, the natural world is green, with the lighting sometimes as stagnant as the hot, humid days. The great treasures of natural color — a rhododendron or a pool of richly hued leaves — come with fall and spring. Working with film, lighting and seasonal variations gives photographers countless challenges and opportunities in their use of nature's colors.

Left: Rhododendron blossoms fill understory, Delaware Water Gap National Recreation Area
Above: Morning light on mossy shore rocks, Cape May

Morning light above the Delaware River, Delaware Water Gap National Recreation Area

Sandy Hook Light at Fort Hancock, Gateway National Recreation Area

Falls and autumn foliage in the Watchung Mountains, Watchung Reservation, Union County

Shoreline of Crater Lake near the Appalachian Trail, Delaware Water Gap National Recreation Area

"Twenty-three kinds of orchids grow in the Pine Barrens
. . . and they are only the beginning of a floral wherewithal
that botanists deeply fear they will someday lose."
— John McPhee, *The Pine Barrens*

Morning light on day lilies, Pine Barrens

Fall forest and Fairview Lake at sunset, from Kittatinny Mountain, Delaware Water Gap National Recreation Area

Red maple tree in bud, Wharton State Forest, Pine Barrens

Clinton Mill reflects in the South Branch of the Raritan River, Clinton
Overleaf: Fall grasses at Round Valley Reservoir, Round Valley State Park, near Lebanon

25

"In the eighteen-seventies, Joseph Wharton, the
Philadelphia mineralogist and financier . . . recognized
the enormous potentiality of the Pine Barrens. . . . The Wharton
Tract, as his immense New Jersey landholding was called,
has remained undeveloped. . . . The state [of New Jersey] was
slow in acquiring it in the public interest, but at last did so
in 1955, and the whole of it is now Wharton State Forest."
— John McPhee, *The Pine Barrens*

Redbud tree in afternoon light, Cheesequake State Park

Batsto Village, a functioning relic of the 18th and 19th centuries, Wharton State Forest, Pine Barrens

Early light on Kittatinny Mountain near the Appalachian Trail, Delaware Water Gap National Recreation Area

Red maple leaves catch light of dawn at Sunrise Point, Stokes State Forest

Autumn ferns, Great Swamp National Wildlife Refuge

Ferns and spring forest, Great Swamp National Wildlife Refuge

FORM

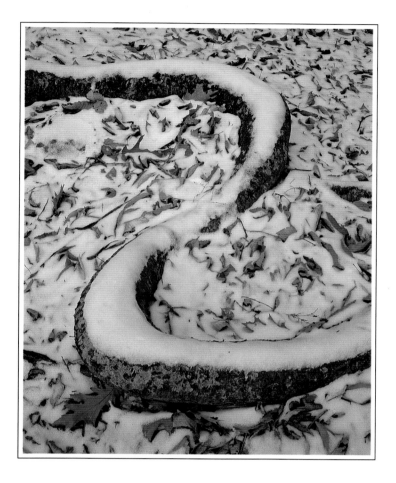

Photographers make a number of conscious and unconscious decisions while creating what they hope will be pleasing images. After looking through a rectangular box for most of my adult life, I use mainly instinct to arrange the forms of my subject into a final composition. At times I may spend hours working or reworking a photograph to simplify or clarify the final result. At other times I run furiously from one opportunity to the next, trying to keep up with the changing face of nature's profuse shows.

Form as revealed in texture is particularly interesting to me in the field. I use film and camera equipment capable of revealing as much detail as possible. I have never been happy with the poor fidelity of reproduction from 35mm films, so I endure the expense and hassle of large equipment to create images that please me.

Pattern in nature is an important aspect of form. All good nature photography can be reduced to the mingling of light and pattern to create form. Patterns can be found in nature that seem almost man-made in their symmetry, while other patterns testify to the chaos of the natural world.

By working with the elements of texture, form, light, color and pattern, photographers have infinite resources to show us the natural world in fresh, fascinating ways.

Left: Sand patterns after autumn storm, Island Beach State Park   Above: Snowy tree root in morning light, Delaware Water Gap National Recreation Area

Sunrise delineates sand patterns, Gateway National Recreation Area

Sunset on swamp snag at Wetlands Institute, near Stone Harbor, Cape May County

"How is it that in all the serenity and lonesomeness of solitude, away off here amid the hush of the forest, alone, or as I have found in prairie wilds, or mountain stillness, one is never entirely without the instinct of looking around . . . for somebody to appear, or start up out of the earth, or from behind some tree or rock?" — Walt Whitman, *Specimen Days*

Glacial erratic along the Summit Trail, Jenny Jump State Forest, New Jersey Highlands

Morning light Batsto Village, Wharton State Forest

"Fine, clear, dazzling morning, the sun an hour high,
the air just tart enough. What a stamp in advance my whole day
receives from the song of that meadow lark perch'd
on a fence-stake twenty rods distant!"
— Walt Whitman, *Specimen Days*

Swamp grasses in snow, Great Swamp National Wildlife Refuge

Ice patterns at South Mountain Reservation, South Orange

"One lesson from affiliating a tree — perhaps the greatest
moral lesson anyhow from earth, rocks, animals, is that same
lesson of inherency, of *what is*, without the least regard
to what the looker on (the critic) supposes or says,
or whether he likes or dislikes."
— Walt Whitman, *Specimen Days*

Morning light on Tripod Rock, a glacial erratic balanced on three smaller rocks, Tripod Rock Reserve

Winter sunset over barren trees, South Mountain Reservation
Overleaf: Dawn mist from Sunrise Point, Stokes State Forest

"Not even an echo; only the cawing of a solitary crow,
flying at some distance. The pond is one bright, flat spread,
without a ripple — a vast . . . glass, in which I study the sky,
the light, the leafless trees, and an occasional crow, with
flapping wings, flying overhead. The brown fields
have a few white patches of snow left."
— Walt Whitman, *Specimen Days*

Swamp snags, Wawayanda State Park

Lone tree in winter fog, Union County

Sunset at Great Falls on the Passaic River, Paterson

Lone feather on beach pebbles, Cape May State Park

49

Hudson Palisades in morning light, Palisades Interstate Park

Weathered barn, Delaware Water Gap National Recreation Area

"
     … our track enter'd a broad region of salt grass meadows,
intersected by lagoons, and cut up everywhere by watery runs.
The sedgy perfume [was] delightful to my nostrils. . . . From
half-past 11 till 2 I was nearly all the time along the beach,
or in sight of the ocean, listening to its hoarse murmur,
and inhaling the bracing and welcome breezes."
               — Walt Whitman, *Specimen Days*

Sunset over Sandy Hook Bay, Gateway National Recreation Area

Flooding stream in Lebanon State Forest, Pine Barrens

STEPHEN TITSWORTH
DIED
June 9th 1859
aged 63 years 5 months
and 8 days

Headstone on winter morning, near Sussex

Laurel blossoms and fallen leaves, Great Swamp National Wildlife Refuge

Snow patterns in Salt Brook, Union County

Vine maple climbs rock wall, Palisades Interstate Park

MOMENT

Fleeting beauties of nature and light are the most difficult and satisfying moments to capture. Nature photographers are sometimes given just seconds to see, compose and physically create a photograph. If I've been in the field for days, my skills and instincts can be especially fine-tuned, while at other times pure luck or lots of patience can help me photograph elusive weather or remarkable light.

While hiking one afternoon I noticed dramatic combinations of dark clouds and winter trees on South Mountain. When I returned an hour later to capture the last and very best light on film, I was disappointed to find the sky clear. As I prepared to leave, another wonderful cloud bank miraculously reformed right at sunset, yielding precisely the shot I wanted. I worked like a dervish, each composition taking seconds to create. Planning and luck allowed me to visualize and photograph an ephemeral event.

Left: Forest in morning fog, Delaware Water Gap National Recreation Area   Above: Evidence of beavers at Crater Lake, Kittatinny Mountain, Delaware Water Gap National Recreation Area

"This is the hour for strange effects in light and shade —
enough to make a colorist go delirious — long spokes of
molten silver sent horizontally through the trees (now in
their brightest tenderest green,) each leaf and branch
of endless foliage a lit-up miracle. . . . "
— Walt Whitman, *Specimen Days*

Great Falls on the flooded Passaic River, Great Falls Park

Catalpa tree and the Delaware River at sunset, Delaware Water Gap National Recreation Area

"A clear, crispy day — dry and breezy air, full of oxygen.
Out of the sane, silent, beauteous miracles that envelope and
fuse me — trees, water, grass, sunlight, and early frost — the
one I am looking at most to-day is the sky. It has that delicate,
transparent blue, peculiar to autumn, and the only clouds
are little or larger white ones, giving their still and
spiritual motion to the great concave."

— Walt Whitman, *Specimen Days*

Snow and stillness frame old boat, Wharton State Forest, Pine Barrens

Evening clouds over Jenny Jump State Forest, near the Summit Trail, New Jersey Highlands

Sunset colors Lake Hopatcong, Bonaparte Point

Autumn fog over the Hudson River, Palisades Interstate Park
Overleaf: Moonset over Wanaque Reservoir, Ramapo Mountains, Ramapo State Forest

"This is the fourth day of a dark northeast storm,
wind and rain. . . . The dark smoke-color'd clouds roll in furious
silence athwart the sky . . . the wind steadily keeps up its hoarse,
soothing music over my head — Nature's mighty whisper."
— Walt Whitman, *Specimen Days*

Foam patterns after storm, Island Beach State Park

Ice floes on the Passaic River, Passaic River Park

Sandy Hook Bay from Fort Hancock, Gateway National Recreation Area

Morning light on icy falls, Delaware Water Gap National Recreation Area

"I don't know what or how, but it seems to me mostly owing to these skies, (every now and then I think, while I have of course seen them every day of my life, I never really saw the skies before,) I have had this autumn some wondrously contented hours. . . . " — Walt Whitman, *Specimen Days*

Morning waves meet shore rocks, near Surf City

Sunrise at Kittatinny Mountain, along the Appalachian Trail, Delaware Water Gap National Recreation Area

"Lights and shades and rare effects on tree-foliage and grass — transparent greens, grays . . . all in sunset pomp and dazzle. The clear beams are now thrown in many new places, on the quilted, seam'd, bronze-drab, lower tree-trunks, shadow'd except at this hour — now flooding their young and old columnar ruggedness with strong light, unfolding to my sense new amazing features of silent, shaggy charm. . . . "
— Walt Whitman, *Specimen Days*

Winter sunset over frozen swamp, Great Swamp National Wildlife Refuge

Rhododendron in snow, Watchung Reservation

PLACE

With an incredible variety of ecosystems and life zones packed into their small area, New Jersey's natural places provide a wonderful representative sampling of the eastern seaboard. Each mountain, each swamp has its own personality and features.

A key element to producing a good image of any place is an affinity for that piece of earth. If I can remember when I look at a finished photograph the way a swamp smelled or the bitter cold I felt on a winter morning, I feel I've been successful. The unique visual qualities I've been able to capture then convey to the viewer a concrete sense of what the place must be like.

Some of the photographs in this book were made at seemingly unremarkable places: roadsides, city parks, urban streams. Even these supposedly nondescript places can provide small flashes of beauty and a reminder of the natural world all around us.

Left: Daffodils and dogwoods in afternoon sunshine, Union County   Above: Water lilies blanket Culvers Lake, near Stokes State Forest

Early spring mosses at Wharton State Forest, Pine Barrens

Sunrise view from Mount Tammany, along the Appalachian Trail, Delaware Water Gap National Recreation Area

Pond reflections at Leonard J. Buck Rock Garden, Somerset County

Falls plunge through narrow notch, Ramapo Mountains

Rushing waters drain Tillman Ravine, near the Appalachian Trail, Stokes State Forest

Morning light on lily pads at Pakim Pond, Lebanon State Forest, Pine Barrens

Late afternoon light on granite boulders, Norvin Green State Forest

Snow-covered rocks in the Raritan River, Ken Lockwood Gorge
Overleaf: Afternoon light on church at Walpack Center, Delaware Water Gap National Recreation Area

Early light in hemlock forest, Tillman Ravine, Stokes State Forest

Primrose blossoms in morning light, Somerset County

"
   . . . I saw the first palpable frost, on my sunrise walk . . .
all over the yet-green spread a light blue-gray veil, giving a
new show to the entire landscape. I had but little time
to notice it, for the sun rose cloudless and mellow-warm,
and as I returned along the lane it had turn'd to
glittering patches of wet." — Walt Whitman, *Specimen Days*

Aftermath of ice storm at dawn, Watchung Reservation

Yellow lady's slipper in afternoon light, Union County

"One of my nooks is south of the barn, and here I am
sitting now, on a log, still basking in the sun, shielded from
the wind. Near me are the cattle, feeding on corn-stalks.
Occasionally a cow or the young bull . . . scratches and
munches the far end of the log on which I sit."
— Walt Whitman, *Specimen Days*

Barn detail at Batsto Village, Wharton State Forest, Pine Barrens

Falls in Van Campen Glen, Delaware Water Gap National Recreation Area

MICROCOSM/ MACROCOSM

Part of the fun of nature photography is that anything of any size is fair game. Between the extremes of closeups and expansive wide-angle views are "intimate landscapes," views of small segments of nature pioneered by master landscape photographer Eliot Porter, who died while the photographs for this book were being made.

Porter perfected the idea of intimate landscapes into an art form of the highest order, allowing us to revel in structure, color and texture. Those who come after him hope to continue his legacy with what he has taught us: the miniature can give us as much to see and understand as the overpowering whole.

New Jersey is not particularly known for large scenic vistas, but with some exploration and often some hiking, I found some marvelous vantage points. Rock outcrops in Norvin Green State Forest stand above the encircling forest, while the ramparts of the Hudson Palisades always provide an inspiring vista. On several occasions I climbed a fire tower in the Pine Barrens, finding the view most beautiful after a wet winter snow. The icy platform was barely big enough for my camera tripod, and the climb up and down as frightening as a western mountain ascent.

Left: Morning light at Kittatinny Mountain, Delaware Water Gap National Recreation Area
Above: Morning light on autumn leaves, Delaware Water Gap National Recreation Area

"Here I am accustom'd to walk for sky views and effects, either morning or sundown. To-day from this field my soul is calm'd and expanded beyond description . . . only sky and daylight . . . the cool dry air . . . the occasional murmur of the wind . . . " — Walt Whitman, *Specimen Days*

Sunset over marshes, Brigantine Unit, Edwin B. Forsythe National Wildlife Refuge, near Atlantic City

Shallow pond at Leonard J. Buck Rock Garden, Somerset County

Fallen azalea blossoms in early light, Somerset County

Shore rocks at Lake Hopatcong, Bonaparte Point

"I sit by the edge of the pond, everything quiet, the broad polish'd surface spread before me — the blue of the heavens and the white clouds reflected from it — and flitting across, now and then, the reflection of some flying bird."

— Walt Whitman, *Specimen Days*

Morning reflections and lily pads, Great Swamp National Wildlife Refuge

Forest floor at sunset, Ringwood State Park, Ramapo Mountains
Overleaf: Wharton State Forest in snow, Pine Barrens

Evening light on marsh marigold, Great Swamp National Wildlife Refuge

Wall of columbines on Kittatinny Mountain, Delaware Water Gap National Recreation Area

"Not a human being, and hardly the evidence of one, in sight. . . . On my walk hither two hours since, through fields and the old lane, I stopt to view, now the sky, now the mile-off woods on the hill, and now the apple orchards. What a contrast from New York's or Philadelphia's streets!"
— Walt Whitman, *Specimen Days*

Evening storm approaches Batsto Lake, Wharton State Forest, Pine Barrens

Morning light on black jack-in-the-pulpit, Somerset County

"After you have exhausted what there is in business, politics, conviviality, love, and so on — have found that none of these finally satisfy, or permanently wear — what remains? Nature remains; to bring out from their torpid recesses, the affinities of a man or woman with the open air, the trees, fields, the changes of seasons — the sun by day and the stars of heaven by night."

— Walt Whitman, *Specimen Days*

Late afternoon light on granite rock face, Norvin Green State Forest

Swamp reflections, Great Swamp National Wildlife Refuge

Sunrise view of the Delaware River from Mount Tammany, along the Appalachian Trail,
Delaware Water Gap National Recreation Area